WHAT IS DESIGN FOR SIX SIGMA?

Other books in McGraw-Hill's "What is...? Series include

What is Sarbanes-Oxley? 0071437967

What is Lean Six Sigma? 007142668X

What is Short Selling? 0071427856

What is Six Sigma? 0071381856

What is Transparency? 0071435484

What is Value Investing? 0071429557

WHAT IS DESIGN FOR SIX SIGMA?

ROLAND R. CAVANAGH
ROBERT P. NEUMAN
PETER S. PANDE

McGraw-Hill

New York Chicago San Francisco Lisbon
London Madrid Mexico City Milan New Delhi
San Juan Seoul Singapore Sydney Toronto

*To all our associates and clients
that provided grist for the mill.*—RRC

Once again for mabel, and for Betty, too.—RN

*To inspired people looking for breakthrough opportunities
in organizations around the world.*—PSP

CONTENTS

BEYOND SIX SIGMA

With books, articles, and case studies pouring in on the effectiveness of Six Sigma across industries, it is clear that the approach has proven itself to be one of the most effective business improvement systems of the last decade. For many who have experienced the power of Six Sigma change, the question arises: "What next?" Now managers and their teams are being asked to go beyond simply improving existing operations and reducing defects. The further challenge is to build Six Sigma levels of excellence into new and renovated processes, products, and services. This book reaches out to the millions of managers and employees whose firms have adopted Six Sigma and are now exploring the more ambitious goal of putting Design for Six Sigma (DFSS) into practice.

DFSS is a proven, robust approach to designing new products and services and redesigning the flaws out of existing offerings. More ambitiously, DFSS can be applied to building new competitive capabilities that go beyond current customer expectations. But DFSS is not easy to understand or apply. This book will help readers understand DFSS by:

- Explaining its role and business impact
- Exploring when and how to apply DFSS
- Introducing companies who have achieved dramatic results with this approach
- Examining the steps of the DFSS process

While this book doesn't replace formal instruction in DFSS methods, it can help prepare, guide, and support anyone who is considering, or is currently part of, a DFSS initiative.

WHAT EXACTLY IS DFSS?

To best understand DFSS, it's helpful to look first at the broader vision and strategies of Six Sigma. While Six Sigma is certainly about solving problems, reducing defects, delighting customers, and boosting profits, it is more than that. The 'big picture" of Six Sigma is about helping an organization and its people make *change a core competency*.

Change is a crucial skill for obvious reasons: Any organization that plans to stay in business for long needs to be good at adapting to new customer demands, changing economic conditions, new technologies, etc. Being *good* at change demands three key capabilities:

1. Knowing *what* to change and when, and then being able to sustain the results (in Six Sigma terms, this is "Process Management").
2. Being able to fix, upgrade, or continuously improve existing processes, products, and services.
3. Having the insight and creativity to create new processes, products, and services and to abandon and redesign those that become obsolete or incapable of meeting current needs (more on capability below).

As you can see in Figure 1.1, methods like DMAIC focus on the improvement strategy, while DFSS is all about designing or redesigning operations and offerings. Both DMAIC and DFSS have their cousins—approaches that can also be applied to improve or design a process. But DMAIC and DFSS are the power tools of business change: They provide the speed, muscle, and discipline needed when significant results are needed.

DFSS builds on the foundation of Six Sigma principles and DMAIC methodology, adding new tools like Quality Function Deployment (QFD) and focusing more heavily on, among other things, Failure Modes and Effects Analysis (FMEA), Design of Experiments (DOE), simulation testing, and design optimization.

DFSS provides a way that users can build quality into processes, products, and services at or close to Six Sigma levels

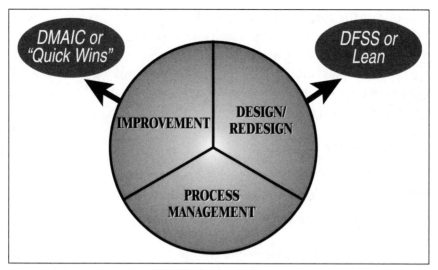

FIGURE 1.1. DMAIC and DFSS compared.

from day one. Yet for practitioners, DFSS is not simply a process or methodology in and of itself; it is a mind-set, an attitude, and a set of tools for designing processes, products, and services that both meet customer expectations and can be produced to near perfection. DFSS is about testing assumptions and exploring exciting new ways to create processes that operate at exponentially higher levels of efficiency and effectiveness.

WHAT YOU'LL LEARN FROM THIS BOOK

If you're reading this, you might already have heard about the impact DFSS has had in companies designing processes, products, and services for a changing market, and have likely been asked to consider incorporating DFSS into your own design methodology as either a project leader or team member. From health care to financial services to manufacturing, DFSS has been effective across a wide range of industries, products, and services. Companies that include Johnson & Johnson, American Express, PriceWaterhouse Coopers, Caterpillar, and DuPont, among others, have accomplished leaps in performance or taken a serious bite out of the rate of new product failure (estimated as low as 40 percent and as high as 80 percent) by applying DFSS methods.

Born from Six Sigma principles, DFSS is founded on four shared characteristics. Whether the design challenge is a new IT system, a core business process, or a new product, DFSS is about ensuring that each newly designed solution:

1. Is customer focused
2. Is defect free
3. Produces major returns on investment
4. Changes how managers operate

Yet DFSS extends from Six Sigma by adding more practical guidelines that drive the ultimate offering towards near perfection:

- Front load the pain. (Establish project goals and deliverables immediately as early as possible to create a clear picture of the scope for the design.)
- Capability—or the ability to consistently perform to customer needs—is the key. (Capability of the entire system, based on understanding and budgeting capability of interfaces and supporting processes.)
- Commit to excellence without compromise.
- Concentrate on communication within your team and with your customers (and don't forget to do your stakeholder analysis).

To summarize, DFSS is about leaping past incremental improvement. Its objective is creating products and processes that are practically immune to problems, that wow customers, and leave employees feeling positive and confident that they can *deliver* value and excellence. DFSS does not try to influence one or two key product features or process steps; it aims to influence practically everything about the product and the way it's produced. (What Six Sigma lovers might call "All the Ys and all the Xs.") If the image of a clean slate or a clear computer screen comes to mind when you think about DFSS, you've got the pic-

RAYTHEON'S SIX SIGMA AND DFSS PRINCIPLES

1. Specify value in the eyes of the customer.
2. Identify the value stream; eliminate waste and variation.
3. Make value flow at the pull of the customer.
4. Involve, align, and empower employees.
5. Continuously improve knowledge in the pursuit of perfection.

Source: http://www.raytheon.com/about/sixsigma/principles. html

Note: While Raytheon's approaches to DFSS and Six Sigma incorporate lean processes, the principles featured above demonstrate how connected these approaches are to the strategic objectives of the company.

ture. It's often a risky undertaking, but one that many companies have chosen and applied with some very dramatic results.

In addition to delving into more depth on what DFSS is, in this book we try to share with you a feeling for a DFSS project, explain the thinking behind selecting projects that would benefit from a design approach, walk you through the DFSS process, and offer techniques and advice that will initiate you into a DFSS team.

DESIGN IT RIGHT THE FIRST TIME: THE IMPACT OF DFSS

D FSS has taken center stage in organizations that span a broad range of industries: financial services, health care, e-learning, technology solutions, and, of course, product development. Through DFSS and Six Sigma, organizations have been able to take their performance to new levels.

Cost savings are typically the first benefit of Six Sigma efforts—but a sustained, customer-driven effort can bring much more impressive rewards. In fact, getting products to market faster, dramatically enhancing the ability to meet specific customer needs, designing in more of the features and benefits demanded by the market, creating processes that support organizational agility and responsiveness—these are the kind of top-line revenue opportunities that can far surpass the benefits of cost cutting.

In designing processes and boosting a company's ability to execute its strategy, DFSS can help reduce the cost, frustration, and frequent disappointment of major information systems initiatives, for instance, and help people break away from the status quo or "the way we've always done things around here."

This chapter details the business impact DFSS has had for a number of companies that have incorporated Six Sigma into the heart of their business strategies and operations. GE has gone so far as to say that Six Sigma has changed the actual DNA of its organization.

A GROWING FORCE, UNTAPPED POTENTIAL

Before looking at benefits and results achieved by Design for Six Sigma, we should touch on the reality around "adoption rates" of DFSS to date. In spite of the commitment made by some leading companies to DFSS methods, use of the design strategies of Six Sigma still lags significantly behind the improvement methods. While DMAIC is in constant use by thousands if not tens of thousands of managers and employees worldwide, DFSS efforts are still found more in pockets.

If the topic of our book is so powerful, why is it slow to be taken up by more companies and people? We've found three key reasons:

1. Most understandably, the number of situations demanding a complete design or redesign of a product, service, or process—versus those requiring improvement—is much lower. No business can operate smoothly if its ongoing operations are in constant overhaul. Improvement of existing activities should always be more common than a total design.

2. Design efforts require a significantly higher commitment and place heavier demands on the resources and talents of the organization. While the potential benefits are much larger, the risk also is greater. As a result, business leaders are more hesitant to launch into a DFSS program or to charter a design project.

3. While one of our goals in this book is to "demystify" Design for Six Sigma, the truth is the design methods of Six Sigma are not explained simply. In fact, DFSS involves shifting your approach to design in meaningful, but often subtle ways in every phase of the design effort. So people investigating DFSS as an option—or individuals brought into a DFSS project—will often ask "exactly how is this different?" Because the answer is not simple, they remain reluctant to give DFSS a try.

WHAT *IS* DIFFERENT ABOUT DFSS?

The following table provides a comparative look at how DFSS upgrades and enhances design efforts, essentially at *every* step in a project. As you'll see when we explore DFSS success stories, the sum of these differences can mean dramatically more successful design efforts.

DESIGN PROJECT TASK OR PHASE	WITHOUT DFSS	USING DFSS PROCESS AND TOOLS
Project Selection	Lack of clear criteria for applying Design or alternate strategy. *Result:* "Design" projects launched that should be improvements, and vice versa.	Clear, well-thought-out decision to apply Design strategy. *Result:* Design is applied only where appropriate, with full recognition of risks and challenges.
Project Definition	Often have unclear objectives and lack of clear direction. *Result:* Projects can drift, with weak cohesion and commitment among key participants.	Emphasis on defining design *Vision*, focusing on compelling and ambitious achievements. *Result:* Projects have clear direction and commitment needed to drive forward in spite of inevitable challenges.
Definition of Design "Outcomes"	Based on what we *think* customers want. New technologies or solutions applied without regard to actual value. *Result:* "Inside-out" design that fails to address real customer or business needs.	Strong emphasis on "Voice of the Customer" data-gathering and analysis. Ideas and designs rechecked with customers over course of design effort. *Result:* "Outside-in" design that emphasizes customer value.
Evolution of Design Specifications	Features, benefits, and design criteria are often fuzzy and subject to change at any time throughout the project.	By "front-loading" a more extensive review of the Vision and customer requirements, specifications are "locked down"

DESIGN PROJECT TASK OR PHASE	WITHOUT DFSS	USING DFSS PROCESS AND TOOLS
Evolution of Design Specifications (cont.)	*Result*: Priorities change constantly, creating delays, higher costs, rework, and frustration among the design team.	earlier. Work can focus on creating and perfecting the process or product that meets the Vision and design criteria. *Result*: Fewer unexpected delays and less rework, greater cohesion among the design team, more effective achievement of the design vision.
Creating and Refining the Design	Elements of the design are often developed in isolation, with each piece focused on being "perfect." Integration of the components is delayed until late in the project schedule. *Result:* Design elements are often "suboptimal," and late integration surfaces problems when little time is left to address them.	Applying a mix of creativity and design integration methods, ideas are surfaced, developed, and tested iteratively earlier in the design cycle. *Result:* Greater coordination among subteams and earlier assessment of the complete design. Good ideas are perfected sooner with fewer "unpleasant surprises."
Design Validation	Frequently shortchanged due to earlier delays in the project. Even when done, little time or few resources are placed on refining the design. *Result:* Defects, bugs, production issues, resistance, etc., are addressed "post-launch."	Heavy emphasis on design testing and risk manage ment, as well as change management to prepare people for the transition. *Result:* Products and processes are "debugged" prior to launch, allowing smoother and less traumatic launches.
Implementation	Design teams work in isolation, developing great ideas that are difficult—even impossible—to execute. *Result:* Major organizational battles between "Designers" and "Users" over whether	Cross-functional efforts ensure that design concepts are communicated to and validated by "operations" as well as external customers or users. *Result:* Designs take into

DESIGN PROJECT TASK OR PHASE	WITHOUT DFSS	USING DFSS PROCESS AND TOOLS
Implementation (cont.)	new products or processes are viable. Also, delays and increased costs in ramp-up as faulty or overly optimistic assumptions are addressed.	account such criteria as manufacturability, serviceability, flexibility, etc. Ramping up or implementing goes much more smoothly.

BUSINESS BENEFITS OF DFSS

Companies that have adopted DFSS practices plan to reach world-class excellence in a variety of functions that span the whole organization. Benefits these companies hope to gain include:

- A thorough understanding of the drivers of customer satisfaction, loyalty, and purchasing decisions that translate into market dominance.
- Improved effectiveness resulting in consistently meeting customer requirements, eliminating defects, and creating "delighters" (those unexpected upgrades that grab a customer's attention and help to build loyalty).
- Enhanced efficiency within the organization by designing streamlined processes that avoid costs due to errors, wasted resources, and rework, thereby maximizing resources.
- Transformed management using analysis and DFSS results to make better decisions in a collaborative environment.

DFSS begins with the essential element crucial to any business regardless of its industry, product, service, or solution: the ability to satisfy specific customer requirements, needs that have been labeled as critical to quality (CTQs).

DFSS does this by bringing the discussion of customer requirements to the forefront of every design initiative and maintains this focus throughout the life of the project. Without DFSS, companies make assumptions about what the customer wants, and processes and design features are more often dictated by cost issues. With DFSS, teams make informed decisions about what requirements are crucial to the customer and verify these decisions through thorough analysis. By adhering to the principles of DFSS, designers create processes that fulfill the customer requirement profitably. This core aspect of DFSS—focusing on the customer—is reflected across the entire design effort—from strategic discussions of how CTQs will enhance the firm's ability to compete in its market to decisions on the best way to roll out the final process or product.

Incorporating this level of customer focus into a business has been the key to managing a thriving company that can withstand shifts in its industry, the marketplace, and economy. Manufacturing and technology companies that include GE, Allied Signal, EDS, and Raytheon have become known as Six Sigma stalwarts, actively promoting the approach within their organizations. And now industries outside of technology are gleaning the benefits of Six Sigma and DFSS. Bank of America is pioneering Six Sigma design among financial services companies after seeing a 22 percent decrease in payment error with a ten-fold increase in payment speed from its efforts. Deposit errors have decreased by 83 percent, and customer satisfaction rose from a baseline of 41 percent to nearly 52 percent, while adding more than 2.5 million customers to the Bank of America family, according to CEO Ken Lewis.

Businesses in the process industries that rely on safe, effective, and customer-driven R&D efforts and are in many cases managed across continents are experiencing the benefits of DFSS in both their operational processes and product lines. One example is DuPont, the number-two chemical maker in the United States and a corporation that manages six distinct businesses. In 1999, the company brought in its first Six Sigma champion, Don Linsenmann, to bring Six Sigma into the strategies and operations of the entire organization. His efforts have been so successful that today one out of every four DuPont employees is involved in a Six Sigma effort, and the company has completed more than 5000 Six Sigma projects. Six Sigma is clearly the focal point of DuPont's multinational business.

In the examples that follow, you'll see how companies were able to break through market downslides, productivity standstills, and innovation stumbling blocks by applying DFSS principles and tactics. Important to the results discussed here are two factors: each company had the support of its most senior management in adopting DFSS, and each was looking for radical, breakthrough improvement as opposed to incremental change.

DFSS IN PRACTICE

CASE 1: DESIGNING THE DFSS PROJECT

A major retailer assembled a cross-functional team to design a way to collect and analyze feedback from their customers at the first point of contact. So, for instance, any time a call center associate heard feedback from a customer, she could somehow capture it and relay it back to the right part of the business. Preliminary process requirements included obtaining real-time data, ensuring the accuracy of data, and correctly analyzing the data so that it was relevant to the firm's business objectives.

One of the primary tools the team used was the House of Quality; the iterative nature of this tool allowed them to analyze the many different customers impacted by the process and prioritize their varying requirements. During the Design stage, the team found the TRIZ brainstorming approach extremely useful, as it provided a new view into the process they were creating. For example, one of the TRIZ categories is "Segmentation," and this team used that concept to segment data and its analysis (e.g., customer segmentation, business segmentation, geographic segmentation, statistically significant versus nonstatistically significant data, etc.) Another TRIZ category is "Replacement of Mechanical System," and the team used that concept to automate data collection, use speech recognition technology, reduce manual inputs, and revise e-mail queues based on priority. You'll learn more about the House of Quality and TRIZ in the discussion of the DFSS toolkit in Chapter 7.

CASE 2: DIVERSIFYING TO MEET CHANGING NEEDS

With the introduction of new fuel emission standards, Cummins, a world leader in the manufacture of large diesel engines, was faced with reducing the volume of N-14 truck engines it manufactured, since its only customers remained in countries where the new standards had not been adopted. This market change caused Cummins to slash its daily output of N-14s in half, ultimately resulting in significant time delays in getting the completed engine off the assembly line. The problem for Cummins was that too many engines were held up as Work-in-Process (WIP) because the assembly line only ran if a certain volume of engines were on it. With the decreased number being produced, it took longer for engines to get through the assembly stage. Cummins needed to reduce the time items spent in WIP.

The company had been using a push flow system in postassembly, so the engines moved from station to station only once a certain volume on the line was reached. Because demand and therefore the volume of N-14s decreased so dramatically, it was difficult to create the kind of volume needed to keep postassembly moving, and as a result Cummins had more engines in WIP than it produced each day.

With the software simulation tool Witness and other DFSS analytical tools, Cummins changed its postassembly process from push flow to pull flow and successfully distributed the work among its carriers so that production was continuous. Through the findings of its Six Sigma team, Cummins made several changes over a four-month period, including reducing the number of carriers it used for the N-14, eliminating unneeded workstations, and reducing extra stages and equipment previously used in postassembly. The result was a 14-percent reduction in throughput time, decreased WIP time of 29 percent, increased productivity of 11 percent, and a cost savings of $268,000.

Using DFSS methods and simulation tools in tandem was crucial to the success of Cummins efforts. The analysis and simulation tools allowed the N-14 production team to see just how the engines were flowing through the process and pinpoint those areas that caused production to stall and engines to go off line. For Cummins, each engine that did not complete production underscored the defects in the company's processes.

CASE 3: KEEPING AHEAD OF OBSOLESCENCE AND A CHANGING INDUSTRY (OR WALKING THE DINOSAUR)

With annual revenues of more than $6 billion and a market cap of $5 billion, Seagate Technology is a leading manufacturer of computer hard drives for electronic systems of all sizes, from personal computers to fully loaded data centers. Under the leadership of then-CEO and current Chairman Steve Luczo, Seagate adopted Six Sigma and DFSS in 1998 in order to defend the company against a decline in the disk-drive industry by increasing customer delight, reducing waste, improving reliability, and reducing time to market. Prior to this, Seagate estimated product delivery on the condition of their manufacturing operations, rather than on the customer's preferred timeframe. (Seagate sells directly to computer manufacturers and distributors, so each customer represents significant potential revenues.)

Initially Seagate applied DFSS to its factory operations with the objective of getting products out to customers before the technology became obsolete—a constant threat in the electronic storage business. Using Six Sigma and DFSS in its Factory of the Future initiative, the company was able to reconfigure operations so that the plant could turn out a new product in a day or two as opposed to what had been weeks in some cases.

Specifically, their analysis showed that among the 200 parts used in its various hard disk drives, only 3 were the same between products. The team used this information and worked with engineers to reduce the variety of parts, and then worked with their outside vendors to do the same while improving on the vendors' delivery times.

From deploying Six Sigma only in their factory, Seagate then applied the approach to the entire organization and achieved their goals of reducing costs and defects. Seagate CEO Bill Watkins reports that at one time the cost of scrap was a significant burden on the company; now, with their streamlined operations, Seagate's shipping costs are a bigger expense than scrap. Since instituting DFSS and Six Sigma in 1998, Seagate estimates that it has saved more than $750 million across 3400 Six Sigma projects.

CASE 4: LOGISTICAL EXCELLENCE

McKesson Corporation is one of the largest pharmaceutical distributors in the United States. The company views its purpose as mission critical. The very nature of its business—supplying life-saving medicines—requires that the ordering system operates at the highest level of accuracy, and that the company maintains an extensive inventory while keeping the medications viable, as well as offer world class logistics for its customers in the United States and Canada. The ability to guarantee customer satisfaction, which in this case means delivering the right medicines on time, is an absolute mandate for McKesson. In fact, pharmaceutical distributors like McKesson are the lifeline for pharmacists, handling approximately $110 billion worth of high-demand drugs, critical medications, and other pharmaceutical products each year. It's an industry that cannot tolerate failure at any level.

McKesson's distribution system, named Acumax, is an award-winning approach that was designed with Six Sigma principles and tools and is a marvel of operational excellence that continuously tracks packages through bar code technology. Acumax exemplifies McKesson's commitment to Six Sigma: The company has used Six Sigma and DFSS to drive process improvements throughout the organization, created a metric-driven culture by tying Six Sigma to both the strategic and operational objectives of the company, and reduced costs for both the customer and McKesson.

Using DFSS methods, McKesson designed integrative features into Acumax that simultaneously allow it to track internal warehousing functions such as receiving, put-away, and order fulfillment at all of its 90 distribution centers and link into the firm's Closed Loop Distribution (CLD) system that uses Palm Pilot technology. The combined investment of Six Sigma and the technology infrastructure represented in CLD/Acumax has McKesson performing with 99.90-percent accuracy.

STARTING DFSS IN YOUR OWN FIRM: THE BASICS OF IMPLEMENTATION

DFSS is not a single technique, but rather a synthesis of tools and approaches that helps overcome the challenges that thwart many design efforts. This synthesis is represented in the five phases of a DFSS project: Define, Measure, Analyze, Design, and Verify (DMADV). DMADV's counterpart in Six Sigma is DMAIC. You'll read more about the comparison between the two in Chapter 3.

These five phases guide a DFSS project from conception to completion and, depending on the goal of the initiative, can take the design team on one of two paths: transforming core business processes or designing strategic breakthrough improvements.

If your organization has fallen behind in key markets, lost profits because new products have failed or were delivered way behind schedule, missed new customer opportunities, or failed to keep up with modern business approaches, then the transformational path is for you.

When DFSS is applied in such cases, you'll be scrutinizing business activities across the firm that can range from how new products are developed and then distributed all the way to the effectiveness of the sales process. Of course, the conventional Six Sigma objectives—decrease defects, eliminate customer complaints, use resources effectively—are considered as well.

If your firm chooses the path of breakthrough improvements, the DFSS team will be asked to focus on specific business needs or specific business units of the organization. These DFSS projects might be just as intense as the transformational ones, but they really aren't as ambitious or wide-ranging as recreating a core business process. On the other hand, many companies begin their DFSS efforts with smaller projects that gradually evolve into a full-scale company initiative as Seagate did.

SUMMARY

It is clear from the brief examples above that DFSS has proven effective in boosting productivity, contributing to cost savings, and increasing time-to-market in industries from e-business to finance to manufacturing. In each segment, innovation is held at a premium and there is little room for wasted resources. When companies incorporate DFSS and Six Sigma into their infrastructure, the impact can be huge.

The following chapter provides a review of Six Sigma basics and a discussion of DMADV as compared with DMAIC. From there, we'll walk you through the DFSS process and discuss next steps for starting a DFSS project in your own firm.

SIX SIGMA BASICS

Understanding DFSS presupposes some knowledge of Six Sigma itself. Because the two approaches are so closely aligned, a brief review of the principles of Six Sigma and its primary improvement method, DMAIC, is probably in order.

SIX SIGMA AS A STATISTICAL MEASURE

The word "sigma" stands for the statistical concept of "standard deviation." Standard deviation in turn is a measure of variation around an average. For example, if we're told that a company's employees have an average yearly income of $50,000 with a standard deviation of $5000, we'd know that there was a good deal of variation in individual salaries, with a small number of people earning as little as $35,000 and about as many earning as much as $65,000. Quite a spread, and one you might not think about if you didn't know the standard deviation.

Six Sigma is a measure of the variation of a process, product, or service from customer requirements. Let's say you run a pizza parlor that offers home delivery to the customer's door within 30 minutes of the time an order is placed with you. Essentially, you are promising to meet three customer requirements: the type of pizza ordered, of course, hot, and within 30 minutes. Here's where Six Sigma comes in as a measure. If you and your crew are late with one pizza delivery out of three, your delivery capability would be measured as Two Sigma. If you improve your process so that 93 out of 100 pizzas arrive steaming at your customers' doorstep, that's a Three Sigma performance, and 7 out of every 100 customers won't be happy or are likely to call back. So what's it take to get a Six Sigma score? 99.9997 percent on-time hot pizzas delivered just the way customers ordered them. Six Sigma is nearly perfect because with this measure we have errors on only three or four pizzas out of one million deliveries.

Levels of Sigma Performance

SIGMA LEVEL	DEFECTS PER MILLION OPPORTUNITIES
6	3.4
5	233
4	6,210
3	66,807
2	308,537
1	690,000

The Six Sigma measure was created to remind us that it is the *customer's* requirements that will always take center stage. Too often businesses concentrate on their own labor costs, internal expenses, and profit levels while downplaying those aspects of their businesses, processes, or products that affect the customer who, after all, defines quality for the company. What they fail to realize is that the sigma measure of variance from customer requirements provides a consistent measure of performance for all aspects of the business. In the pizza delivery example, the sigma measure takes into account the order-taking process, the preparation and cooking process, and finally the delivery process.

In this example, we said that customers had three crucial requirements: the correct pizza, delivered on time, and hot. In sigma terms, we identify these requirements as being Critical to Quality (CTQ) as defined by the customer. We might put a nice bow around the delivered pizza box, but why bother? It's not a critical requirement. These CTQ requirements become the foundation for all measures in DFSS.

SIX SIGMA AS A GOAL

When a pizza parlor or any other business fails to meet crucial customer requirements, it creates extra costs and unhappy customers. We call these failures to meet CTQ requirements "defects," and the goal of Six Sigma is to reduce the number of these defects to the vanishing point. These defects cost money in one form or another—refunds, rebates, rework, replace, reship, recall—you won't find these costs in any company's business plan, but they happen every day in companies saddled with defects.

HOW LOW CAN YOU AFFORD TO GO?

1 Sigma   For every 1 million tax returns, 691,500 will be mis-calculated.

2 Sigma   For every 1 million bank statements, 308,537 will be wrong.

3 Sigma   For every 1 million lab results, 66,807 will be in error.

4 Sigma   For every 1 million airplane engines, 6210 will be faulty.

5 Sigma   For every 1 million meals served, 233 will be inedible.

The cost of defects and the rework needed to fix them amounts to nearly a quarter of many businesses' sales. This stark figure should encourage more businesses to set the near perfect target of Six Sigma as their goal. (And let's not leave the government out of this sad picture. An article in the *Wall Street Journal* of September 4, 2003 reported that "Internal Revenue Service employees at tax-help centers gave correct answers to just 57% of tax-law questions asked by Treasury Department investigators posing as taxpayers." This sorry number translates to 1.7 Sigma, meaning that hundreds of thousands of taxpayers are getting incorrect answers to their questions.) Low sigma numbers translate to high levels of rework expenses and other related costs.

Like all lofty goals, Six Sigma requires considerable effort and time to achieve. Complex processes and products might need years of incremental improvement to approach such high levels. Such efforts should be reserved for the handful of key products, processes, and services that directly contribute to meeting customer requirements. We won't need to reach Six Sigma on the daily lunch specials in our company cafeteria, unless, of course, our customers eat there and require only the very best!

SIX SIGMA AS A SYSTEM OF MANAGEMENT

When asked why his company was doing Six Sigma, one of our client CEOs answered, "Because I can't think of anything else to do! I closed down warehouses and sold off parts of the business that weren't worth keeping, consolidated this function with that, and laid off a bunch of people—all obvious fixes. Now I've really got to start managing the business and Six Sigma is the best thing I know of. You got a better idea? Let me know what it is."

This CEO's gruff honesty is common among managers in Six Sigma companies, and among their employees, too. Six Sigma is not simply a way to do "quality" or "customer service; it's actually a way to manage the business differently. As a management system, Six Sigma emphasizes six themes that are also the primary tenets of DFSS:

1. Genuine Focus on the Customer

Companies beginning a Six Sigma program quickly discover how little they really know about their customers. With Six Sigma, customer focus is the top priority. Problems are defined as failures to meet customer requirements, and projects are chosen for their potential to meet and exceed those requirements.

2. Data and Fact-Driven Management

In the age of information technology and the learning organization, many businesses still manage a lot by instinct and out-of-date assumptions. Perhaps these methods work on occasion, but they can be disastrous when used all of the time. Six Sigma managers operate on a steady, reliable stream of current data about their products, their processes, and their customers.

3. Focus on the Process

One of the great breakthroughs for Six Sigma managers is the ability to understand how a process operates; the step-by-step way in which goods and services are delivered must be one of their central concerns, second only to the needs of customers. Hence, Six Sigma managers don't waste time exhorting the troops to do better; rather, they measure, analyze, and improve core processes.

4. Proactive Management

Six Sigma managers are as good at preventing fires as their predecessors were at putting fires out. Proactive management means preventing problems from happening by performing the routine but effective jobs of planning, gathering feedback, taking measures, and meeting goals.

5. Boundaryless Collaboration

Boundaryless collaboration is a term coined by General Electric based on one simple insight; we all work for the same company and for the same reason: to make a profit by meeting customer requirements as efficiently and effectively as possible. Once we're clear on these fundamentals, all of the fuss about job descriptions and "reporting relationships" and "turf" are revealed for what they can sometimes become: time-wasting distractions from the real business of serving the customer.

6. Driving Toward Perfection, Tolerating Honest Failure

On the road to being right 99.9997 percent of the time, there will be honest failures. People will try their best to find the cause of problems and risk the creation of new products or new processes. They won't always be right the first time, but with the help of DFSS, the chances for failure are sharply diminished.

WHERE SIX SIGMA CAN TAKE YOU

Now that you know a little more about Six Sigma, it's time to outline where you can go with it. Although the goal of extreme quality remains the same, the paths to that goal are sometimes quite different. To illustrate the possibilities, let's stick with our earlier pizza parlor example.

Let's say that your pizza business has been booming for the last couple of years—thanks in part, of course, to your strong focus on customer requirements. You added two pizza ovens to the original one you started with so you can cope with the peak demands on Friday, Saturday, Sunday, and Monday nights. Things were going well until three weeks ago, when some customers started complaining that their pizzas were being delivered half-baked and doughy instead of with the crisp crust they'd ordered. You never had this problem before, and when you asked your employees what might be causing the problem, nobody had a clue.

Now, if you had to deal with this problem, what would you hope to do? Probably you want to find the cause or causes of the sticky pizzas, eliminate those causes, and get back to the business of making money by making customers happy with their hot, crispy pizzas delivered on time. You'll need to know what changed in your process about three weeks ago. What caused those crusts to be doughy and half-baked? *Your goal is to get back to the way things were before the problem appeared, not necessarily to create a whole new way of cooking and delivering pizza.* The method of finding and eliminating the causes of problems like this *is one of the* ways of applying the Six Sigma *improvement method* called DMAIC. DMAIC is an acronym for the phases in a Six Sigma effort.

DEFINE the problem, the process, and the customer requirements not being met.

MEASURE the extent of the problem by gathering data from your process, your product, and your customers.

ANALYZE the data and the process to find out what's causing the problem.

IMPROVE the process by eliminating the causes and building in safeguards to make sure the problem doesn't return.

CONTROL the new solution by taking regular measures and checking routinely on its operation, identifying opportunities for further improvements.

Think of the DMAIC process as a way of making incremental improvements in processes and products. The DMAIC motto might be "Easy does it. One step at a time." First you'll use it to investigate special problems like the half-baked pizzas that suddenly started showing up a few weeks ago. Once these are eliminated, and you still want to make some further improvements but nothing too drastic, you might want to reduce the variation in some of the common daily operations—the amount of water added to the pizza flour, the exact time pizzas spend in the oven, their position in the ovens during peak order time, oven temperatures, and so on.

Managers apply DMAIC in order to solve a problem in their processes, products or services; their goal is to methodically dig out and eliminate the causes of their problems. This is where the similarities between DMAIC and DFSS begin to diverge. DFSS is not designed for incremental improvement; instead its goal is to create a new process, product, or service that is defect free from Day One and beyond. Perhaps this is the reason that many Six Sigma professionals and practitioners identified DFSS as one of their biggest challenges. A recent survey conducted by *Quality Digest* subscribers and online members showed that many companies reach a brick wall with their Six Sigma efforts at Five Sigma and stay stuck at that level.[1] DFSS provides a way to break this barrier by building a process that is completely error free and operating at Six Sigma from Day One. The stumbling block is that few Six Sigma practitioners are trained in DFSS. One of the goals of this book is to provide enough information to give you a head start in your DFSS training.

---

[1] "Six Sigma Survey," *Quality Digest*, February 2003, www.qualitydigest.com/feb03/articles/01_artilces.shtml

CHAPTER 4

THE PROCESS BEHIND THE ACRONYM

Just as DMAIC represents the steps in a Six Sigma effort, DMADV is one of handful of acronyms used to describe the stages of a DFSS project. In this chapter we'll review the language of DFSS.

DMADV, the most common acronym in use today, was first coined by General Electric to describe their vision of the steps needed to accomplish a Six Sigma design. DMADV stands for Define, Measure, Analyze, Design, and Verify. At the broadest level, it means identifying and clarifying what will be worked on, deciding how it will be measured, analyzing the situation, detailing the design, and testing and deploying the new process, product, or service.

DEFINE

The DEFINE phase clarifies customer requirements. It encompasses two core themes of DFSS and establishes the foundation for the remaining phases. The first two themes, Understand the Customer's Needs and Front-Load the Pain, are reflected in a process and tools that are not very different from those used in the Define phase of a Six Sigma improvement project. The areas of greater emphasis and specific outcome of the Design phase in a DFSS project reflect the need to understand *all* of the requirements that the final design must satisfy, and to gain consensus on the product or service design generations.

The Define phase is broken into three parts: the first, Chartering, creates an understanding of and agreement with the

Project Charter, a Job Description that defines several crucial issues. Above all, this phase creates a vision of what success will look like. Further, the Charter clarifies the purpose, scope, and constraints of the task at hand, the roles and responsibilities of the various participants, and outlines a preliminary project schedule.

The second part of the Define phase, Voice of the Customer, is perhaps the most underestimated aspect of DFSS. It is dedicated to gathering, consolidating, sorting, ranking, and verifying the requirements that are Critical to Quality for customers (usually referred to as CTQs). These CTQs need to be balanced against business constraints such as cost, time, and links to business strategy. The outcome of this work is a design document. This document contains the complete list and description of what the new design must accomplish. This is where the customer's voice speaks the loudest and becomes integrated with internal business requirements (such as manufacturability or controllership). This document is the guiding reference for the entire design process.

The purpose of the third part of the Define phase, High-Level Mapping, is to catalog the processes that are affected by or will support the project. In addition to clarifying the processes involved in the project, these processes are mapped out at a high level and begin to build the foundation for establishing a measurement system.

Most DFSS training workshops include a short section at the end of the Define phase devoted to making the project more manageable—that is, attempting to break it into smaller, more bite-sized deliverables or generations, each with its own vision of success. Some courses also include discussion and tools to anticipate and manage team behaviors during crucial project activities.

MEASURE

In a design project, the Measure phase is all about developing future measures of success and establishing tolerance (or margin analysis) and budgeting. The bulk of the work in the Measure phase lies in identifying the appropriate aspects to measure and deciding how they will be evaluated. For a product design, this means selecting the crucial features of the new product and determining how will they be evaluated. In a process design, the team will identify possible future errors and devise ways to prevent them from happening.

In the Measure phase, the flow of work is often different if dealing with a Product/Process development versus Process only. Not only must there be measurements for the product being developed, correlated measures must be devised for the process that will actually create the new product. For example, if a new industrial cooker being designed must be able to withstand pressures of over 2000 pounds per square inch, the process needed to build this cooker must itself have gauges that measure the thickness of the metal walls of the cooker, to predict their ability to withstand such high pressures.

ANALYZE

ANALYZE involves creating innovative concepts for the new product or service that will identify how each step in the process contributes its share to the overall performance of the product or process. The result is an "allowance" or tolerance for each dimension, feature, or step.

This part of the Analyze phase challenges assumptions and tests paradigms, and combined with creative thinking, should result in a narrowed list of concept proposals.

DESIGN

The DESIGN phase details the list of design alternatives, selects the best of the best, and then focuses on testing, testing, testing. Whether designing a product or a process, the Design phase is the time to add flesh to the bones of the conceptual proposals. Now the focus is on the details. Remember when we said that Six Sigma was primarily about discipline and commitment? This phase is where those qualities are tested; teams will need discipline to do the detail work and commit to all of the DFSS principles. Once the remaining alternative ideas are described in sufficient detail, each is evaluated for failure-resistance, predicted capability, and impact on the CTQs. The ideas are then simulated and tested as a prototype in a final effort to select the best design option.

VERIFY

VERIFY, the testing and deployment phase, is similar to the Control phase of a Six Sigma project except that it is preceded by additional testing and optimization. This step ensures that all the necessary documentation, monitoring systems, and response plans are put in place before the launch.

VARIATIONS ON DMADV

So what's different about the other DFSS acronyms? Generally not very much, except for some variations in the organization of the tools that might emphasize certain sections of the work, be customized to fit the culture and lingo of the company, or be changed to differentiate one consulting firm from another. GE, for instance, now refers to their DFSS process as DMADOV, adding the Optimize phase between Design and Verify to make the optimization effort explicit. Several years ago at GE Capital Services there was an expectation that a DFSS project using the DMADV process would be followed by additional improvement efforts. In reality this initiative resulted in less than optimal initial designs as compared to the project goals. GE's Corporate VP of Six Sigma, Piet van Abeelen, recently referred to DMADV as "Six Sigma for poets," meaning that it was lightweight and too theoretical. To counteract this "gotta get something out fast, we'll clean it up later" attitude, adding a separate phase, with its schedule contribution and some kind of tollgate review, makes this important bit of work unavoidable.

Define, Customer, Concept, Design, and Implement (DCCDI), popularized by Geoff Tennant of Mulbury Consulting Limited, features the following steps: The project goals are Defined; Customer analysis is completed; Concept ideas are developed, reviewed, and selected; Design is performed to meet the customer and business specifications; Implementation is completed to develop and commercialize the product/service.

Identify, Design, Optimize, and Verify (IDOV): Identify the customer and specifications (CTQs). Design translates the customer CTQs into functional requirements and into solution alternatives. (A selection process whittles down the list of solutions to the "best" solution.) Optimize with advanced statistical tools and modeling to predict and upgrade the design and performance. Validate ensures that the design you've developed will meet customer CTQs.

Define, Measure, Explore, Develop, and Implement (DMEDI): Although it is being popularized by financial services companies, Caterpillar has also had great success with this approach. Like the alternative models, DMEDI exploits QFD tools to translate customer needs into design requirements, but the Develop stage makes use of lean Six Sigma tools and simulation techniques in order to create a robust design.

While DFSS acknowledges a number of various methods, the constants are its focus on using QFD to establish design requirements that take into account customer priorities and including advanced design tools in the process such as Failure Modes and Effects Analysis, benchmarking, Design of Experiments, simulation, and error proofing, among others.

The following chapter looks at how DFSS is actually applied.

CHAPTER 5

HOW TO APPLY DFSS

When applied rigorously, DFSS improves profits. As we've seen in earlier chapters, DFSS projects focus on either transforming a core business process within the organization or designing a new service or innovative product. This chapter discusses the primary elements of a DFSS project, describing the nature of the project (Greenfield or redesign), and focusing on ways the organization can galvanize around the project in order to ensure its success.

WHAT GETS DESIGNED

As either a brand new project (Greenfield) or a redesign of an existing process or product, DFSS basically uses the same principles and toolkit throughout the entire DMADV process. First, Voice of the Customer (VOC) techniques are applied to establish the project's CTQs and then confirm the robustness of the design during the delivery phase of the project, whether the project focuses on tangible products or intangible services and processes.

Tangible product design or redesign refers to designing a physical thing, whether it's a newly designed computer chip or a redesigned locomotive. In both cases, the DFSS team must gather customer requirements through VOC techniques and then incorporate these CTQs into their new design.

If the DFSS team is focusing on a new service offering (an intangible in that it can't be physically held in your hands), everything from a new type of financing, insurance benefits, or even spa services, the design process might be a little more complex. There are typically many more touches, more customer

---

"GREENFIELD" VERSUS REDESIGN

Redesigns differ from Greenfield designs because the redesigns carry the baggage of the existing product or process. This baggage takes two forms: the first is typically an abundance of VoC, both positive and negative, that can either provide the foundation for an expanded VoC effort or constrain the design to Customer "must-haves" (at the expense of discovering "delighters"); the second form of baggage carried by a redesign is the tendency for the team members to be caught in the current paradigm, unable or unwilling to consider alternatives or get "out of the box." It is often recommended that redesign teams should take a "Greenfield" approach (don't study the old design, rather start with a clean sheet of paper) to avoid these constraints.

---

delighters, in a service offering—from the first call to find out what type of benefits are offered under the insurance coverage, to matching the right benefits package with the individual patient, and finally processing the bills correctly. Most important to remember is that when designing services that operate at Six Sigma levels, the VOC is absolutely vital.

A particularly influential concept of VOC dates back to 1987, when Jan Carlzon, president of Scandinavian Airlines System (SAS) at the time, revealed his notion of "moments of truth," where customers were left with an impression of the quality of service they had just received. In his book appropriately titled *Moments of Truth*, Carlzon explained how he turned his failing airline into a profitable business by focusing on the moments in time where SAS directly interacted with its customers. Whenever a customer interaction took place, whether it was a question asked, a ticket purchased, a bag checked, or a flight canceled, a moment of truth occurred, and from that customers decided whether or not their own requirements had been met. Carlzon calculated that SAS had some 50 million moments of truth a year, each lasting about 15 seconds. Each moment, he said, was "an opportunity to earn a loyal customer" or to lose one.

Carlzon's rules still hold true today, only more so. Moments of truth have multiplied exponentially because they now occur around the clock and in all media, traditional and digital. Moments of truth can involve live interactions between consumers and brand representatives, or automated interactions using the mail, the Web, PDAs, and automated phone systems. No matter where or when it occurs, if a moment of truth fails to satisfy the customer's requirements, that customer can be lost. But if a moment of truth produces a response that satisfies customer requirements—then a moment of *trust* is created. Customers can trust the process to meet its requirements regularly.

When design teams are intent on transforming a business process, they focus on every moment in which the customer— whether internal or external to the company—comes into contact with the organization. Whether contracting and paying suppliers on time, distributing information systems that link the functional departments of the company, or instituting new pricing models, each effective process reflects the organization's focus on excellent service or so-called moments of trust where high-quality processes perform well each time, in every location.

ORGANIZING AROUND THE DFSS PROJECT

The aim of the DFSS team is to create things that will always meet customer requirements, and sometimes delight customers with unexpected pleasant surprises. To achieve these aims, the design team must have the support not only of a Six Sigma champion, but also of the organization as a whole, which means that the firm's executives, officers, and directors must be willing to modify operations and culture to sustain the DFSS effort. These senior managers assume a strategic perspective of the DFSS operation, ensuring that the teams are working on the right projects at the right time so that their efforts bring the most value to the company. But identifying the right projects is only the first step; management must not be afraid to reevaluate how it develops new products and processes and not hesitate to make fundamental changes if the environment is not already Six Sigma friendly. Very often, these changes will begin with customer surveys and data collected by the sales and marketing team.

To implement DFSS effectively, managers must accept the following responsibilities:

1. Establish requirements early in the design process: customer data gathering must occur at all functional levels within the organization, and CTQs must be given to the design team early in the process. So while the team is building technical capabilities into the product, they are also considering CTQs from marketing, sales, and purchasing and any other department involved with the new product.

2. Provide more resources early on: plan on needing 15 percent to 25 percent additional resources beyond the baseline plan in order to optimize the early stage of the design process by effectively identifying CTQs, transferring requirements to the design, and coming up with robust yet innovative design concepts.

3. Develop product platforms: Think beyond a project-by-project basis for your company's DFSS initiatives and develop product suites or platforms using the approach. Developing product platforms can provide strategic advantage for an organization in a variety of areas from branding through multiple distribution channels.

4. Assume the champion's role: for DFSS to deliver on its promises, the organization needs managers who themselves are Six Sigma champions. In this role, management needs to fully understand the DFSS process, its tools, and the environment needed to achieve the best results. Management must make changes where needed and communicate these changes so each employee understands how DFSS will impact the company and job requirements As champions, managers will be called upon to provide leadership, generate vision, provide resources, monitor results, and map out other uses for DFSS that will bring Six Sigma effectiveness to the entire organization.

PROCESS DESIGN AND REDESIGN FOR DFSS

Imagine that you're dealing with a problem with your house, the problem being that you don't have enough room. You could jump immediately to one single solution and start looking for a new home, but perhaps you're more cautious and logical than that. Before buying a new house, you want to be sure that this is the best solution for your problem. Maybe you don't need a new house at all. Perhaps you have enough space buried under all the stuff you've loaded in over the last 15 years. Maybe all you need to do is run a month's worth of rummage sales and then store the remainder neatly.

Our natural fascination with brand-new things tempts us to immediately adopt a DFSS approach (a model intended to result in large-scale change, as opposed to the incremental results of Six Sigma and DMAIC). But these tendencies need to be resisted and a project design or redesign undertaken only if one of two conditions exist:

Condition #1: When a major threat, opportunity, or need exists.

Condition #2: When your firm is in a position to take on the risk of a DFSS project.

THE BENEFITS OF DFSS

The opportunity for DFSS might arise out of various customer or organizational needs or threats to the company. Some of the situations where new product design or redesign is needed include:

Changing marketplace needs: Whether new demands arise from evolving customer bases or shifts in the industry, this new market environment will impact the sustainability of your firm. If your products, services, or processes are not capable of meeting new marketplace demands or are not flexible enough to handle a wide range of needs and requirements, DFSS is in order.

New technologies: Technological advances that impact a firm's product, services, or methods of operation should drive interest in a design or redesign effort, lest the company's portfolio of offerings and way of conducting business becomes obsolete.

New or changed rules and regulations: Like the Cummins example of the N-14 truck engine discussed in Chapter 2, changing standards and regulations often force companies to respond quickly and decisively. These types of sudden changes can eat up a less disciplined organization. At Cummins the company was able to keep making the engine for international customers who were not affected by new regulations.

Old assumptions: Whether old competitors are gaining an edge, new entrants are fragmenting your markets, customer trends are sneaking up on you, human resources processes are changing the workforce landscape, or any combination of these, there is a terrible pressure on businesses to keep their strategies fresh and their operations cutting-edge. This is just how General Electric, Allied Signal, and a host of other leading organizations used Six Sigma and DFSS and achieved notable results.

CAN YOU HANDLE DFSS?

Much like the decision-making process that will resolve the housing problem we started with, a similar logic is followed when considering the use of DFSS to create new processes or products. In the case of the house, you need to decide what the extra room is for: is there too much mess, or are you adding a home office? Solutions for the former (garage sales, closet consultants, storage equipment) won't help the latter.

The same type of assessment exercise is used when considering project design or redesign. Here are some of the questions you and your team should consider when thinking about DFSS as opposed to DMAIC.

Has the Existing Product or Process Reached Its Full Capacity?

Before embarking on DFSS, a process or product must be carefully measured to see how well it is meeting customer requirements. If the gap is close, some minor adjustments and small increments might break the entitlement barrier (the point at which the process or product has reached its full capability and cannot be improved). If the gap between what customers want and what is delivered is too large, however, you have to ask if the old product will ever go beyond entitlement. If you require a top speed of 100 miles an hour, there's not much point in tinkering with gear ratios or lighter alloys on your bicycle. If the bike reaches its full capacity or entitlement at a much lower speed, no amount of tinkering will meet the speed requirement. Time for DFSS—or a car! Either way, drastic action is in order.

Estimating the capacity of the new product or process also carries some risk because it involves nearly as much art as science. In the case of a product, we must estimate the performance levels of product components; for the process, the operation of a family of subprocesses needs to be taken into account, and then DFSS teams must make a stab at predicting the new performance level. A well-designed experiment might provide the needed predictive data.

Do We Have Time for DFSS?

Obviously it takes longer to build a house than it does to paint one. In DFSS, much of the building time is devoted to an exhaustive analysis of customer requirements and their translation into design concepts, more time than might be spent in an incremental improvement using the DMAIC process. New designs also require carefully planned and measured pilots. And the list goes on. Before undertaking a DFSS venture, make sure you can afford the 6 to 12 months or more that many such projects require. If not, consider whether or not the project could be broken into a number of phases with shorter timelines.

CAN WE ACCEPT THE RISKS THAT COME WITH DFSS?

Because we're going to create something quite new, the risk of failure or of taking too long increases. There must be a high level of support from management for DFSS as well as a tolerance for unavoidable errors and setbacks along the way. Without these high levels of support, it's probably best to stick to step-by-step improvements. Included in the risk, of course, is the cost of DFSS. While DFSS increases the chances of producing a better-quality product, service, or process, it does not eliminate prototype failures along the way. Innovation has many uncertainties, and cost is one of them.

Other common design pitfalls include misjudging the scope of the project, having incomplete or faulty customer data, or testing the design too late in the process. The impact of these and other pitfalls of design efforts range from fairly minor project delays to complete failure to meet the needs of the customer. Also a surprise to some people is the degree to which a design project's success depends on your ability to "sell" the design, to gain support from key individuals. Having the vision in place early in the project can make it easier to drive support and keep team members inspired.

COMMON DESIGN PITFALLS

Scope of the project is too big.

Vision and goals were not clearly defined early in the process.

Customer input is not clear or is incomplete.

Detailed design work begins too soon.

Piloting or testing of the design begins too late.

Ineffective championing of the design occurs.

Design vision is lost in the details.

Ways to measure or assess the success of the project are not clear.

GETTING STARTED

DFSS allows you to systematically and methodically integrate tools, methods, processes, and team members in order to build Six Sigma quality into your products, services, and processes. While DFSS efforts vary dramatically from company to company, most efforts follow the same road map, typically starting with a charter (linked to the organization's strategic plan), an assessment of customer needs, functional analysis, identification of CTQs, concept selection, detailed design of products and processes, and control plans.

The beginning of the process centers on identifying the Voice of the Customer, using tools such as Value and Cycle Time Analysis and Quality Function Deployment (QFD). From this, DFSS goals are assessed and measures assigned, designs are initiated, and the appropriateness of the new product or process analyzed and verified. Figures 6.1 and 6.2 lay out the DMADV road map and its associated goals and tools, and the next chapter discusses the DFSS toolkit in greater detail.

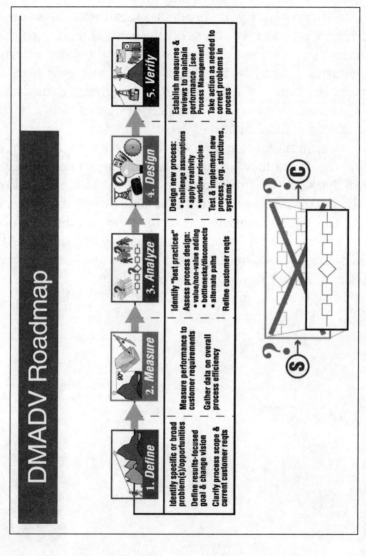

DMADV Roadmap

1. Define

Identify specific or broad problem(s)/opportunities

Define results-focused goal & change vision

Clarify process scope & current customer reqts

2. Measure

Measure performance to customer requirements

Gather data on overall process efficiency

3. Analyze

Identify "best practices"

Assess process design:
• value/non-value adding
• bottlenecks/disconnects
• alternate paths

Refine customer reqts

4. Design

Design new process:
• challenge assumptions
• apply creativity
• workflow principles

Test & implement new process, org. structures, systems

5. Verify

Establish measures & reviews to maintain performance [see Process Management]

Take action as needed to correct problems in process

FIGURE 6.1. The DMADV road map.

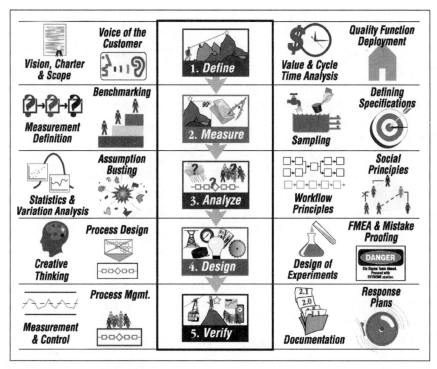

FIGURE 6.2. The entire process.

THE DFSS TOOLKIT: DESIGNING WHAT THE CUSTOMERS REALLY WANT

If you're like most people, you probably have a toolbox in the garage containing a large number of tools, but you only use a handful of them regularly. The same is true of the DFSS toolbox: There are many different tools, designed for different purposes, but there are 10 or so that are used on practically every DFSS project. This chapter focuses on these basic tools, describing what they are and how you might use them within the DMADV framework.

TOOLS FOR THE DEFINE PHASE

KANO ANALYSIS

Understanding customer requirements is fundamental to Six Sigma, and is the core of any DFSS project. Much effort is invested in gathering, clarifying, and classifying the anticipated customer's requirements because these CTQs will ultimately drive the design of the offering. The Kano model (named after Dr. Noriaki Kano, a Japanese management professor and quality expert) offers a way of categorizing requirements very early in the DFSS process as either Must Haves, Satisfiers, or Delighters.

Must Haves (or Dissatisfiers) are the features that customers have come to expect in the product or service, those basic attributes whose absence will cause customer dissatisfaction. For example, guests in a hotel expect clean towels in their room on arrival. They take the presence of clean towels for granted. Missing or dirty towels, on the other hand, will dissatisfy the hotel guest. DFSS innovations must always meet basic customer requirements, and whenever they can, exceed them or even delight customers with the unexpected.

Satisfiers are features that can increase or decrease the level of customer satisfaction to the degree to which they either meet or don't meet customer requirements. For example, having several very large bath towels might be more satisfying to most hotel guests than a larger amount of standard-size towels. DFSS projects should consider the impact on customer satisfaction of increasing the impact of existing features.

Delighters are unexpected features and services that impress customers and put you in the bonus round. For example, having a thick bathrobe to relax in after a shower might delight a weary hotel guest. Where feasible, DFSS projects should include delight features that encourage repeat business without sacrificing profitability.

While DFSS projects try to excel in all three of Kano's categories, Must Haves are usually easiest to identify because they already exist within the customer's experience either as a result of an earlier need that was not met or a superior offering from a competitor. This feedback is given free of charge as complaints and comments (and, occasionally, kudos) and requires translation into criteria that are CTQs. Must Haves, as their name implies, cannot be disregarded during the design effort. For example, warm cookies on the hotel check-in counter won't offset a missing room reservation!

Satisfiers come from either our own or our customer's experience and can be found in complaints as well as from customer surveys. Satisfiers also need to be addressed by the new design before the delighters are added. It is difficult to remain impressed with the free high-speed Internet service in a hotel room if the television is tiny and the number of channels limited.

Delighters represent the added value that will solidify your place in the market and grow your customer base. Data collection techniques like focus groups, or more specifically, innovation groups, can be structured to target delighters that lie beyond the customers' experience. No customer asked Chester Carlson for a Xerox copier when he patented his original idea in the 1930s, but customers were delighted with the product when the machines finally came on the market in 1959.

Gathering and listing customer requirements are typically done early in every DFSS project. Asking the customers to classify them according to the three Kano categories is usually a part of the Define step in DMADV, and identifying an imbalance among them is reason for additional information gathering.

CONJOINT ANALYSIS

Conjoint Analysis is another way of further defining and clarifying the Voice of the Customer (VOC) by prioritizing the relative importance of customer requirements. Many times there are trade-offs made when choosing between requirements, based on multiple criteria. Conjoint analysis can help decode and quantify this trade-off. It works by suggesting quality features to customers via surveys or focus groups in which they are asked which combination of features or what level of service best meets their requirements.

A common example is the conflicts between various CTQs for airline flights. Consider an airline trying to put together a profile of customer requirements on round-trip flights between Sacramento and Denver. Customers might be given a combination of service offerings and levels of service like the following, and then asked to state their preference for them on a scale of one to nine, where nine is most preferable:

1. As an airline passenger, I would prefer: Normal legroom/$400/meal service/no in-flight movie.
2. As an airline passenger, I would prefer: Normal legroom/$400/no meal service/in-flight movie.

The resulting analysis delivers scores reflecting the relative importance of the individual services and levels of service. Software is readily available to make the inquiry process more automatic and to directly deliver the scores. Some software contains intelligence to discontinue the survey where a strong preference is exhibited early in the data collection, significantly reducing the time a customer spends responding to your questionnaire. With proper sampling, and well-constructed service and feature questions, conjoint analysis tools used during the Define stage can provide data on how customer preferences are ranked.

QUALITY FUNCTION DEPLOYMENT

Technically, Quality Function Deployment (QFD) is not really a tool, rather it is an overall approach by which customer requirements are linked to and realized in the new products and services being created to meet those requirements. This method is first used to Define customer requirements, but is then deployed in all phases leading up to and including Design.

QFD is accomplished via a series of interlocking matrices (called "rooms") that connect and deploy customer needs to design requirements or high-level product features, as shown in Figure 7.1. In turn, other grids review the relationships among the high-level features, while others evaluate design features against competitors and various technical benchmarks. The final output of the "House of Quality" is a list of specific, measurable performance targets for the yet-to-be brainstormed new product, service, and process. Although the House of Quality is fairly elaborate, its ability to convert fairly vague customer needs like "I want healthy food" into a very precise specification for a new snack like "Product should contain no more than 3 percent fat" makes it a widely used tool in the Define stage of DFSS.

Later, when the team has brainstormed and experimented with new products, it will measure its effectiveness in meeting customer requirements against the specifications emerging from the House of Quality.

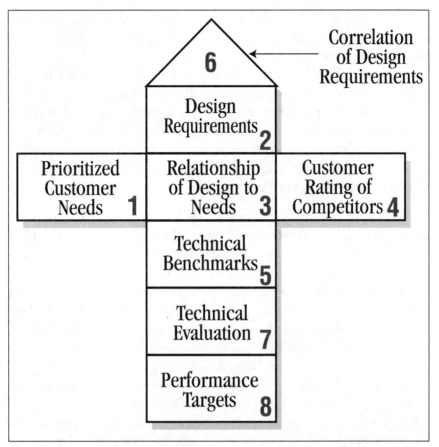

FIGURE 7.1.   QFD "House of Quality."

TOOLS USED IN THE MEASURE PHASE

BENCHMARKING

Precise customer requirements are not the only source of ideas for new products and services. These ideas can come from comparisons or "benchmarks" with other suppliers of similar products, or even with those considered "best in class." Technically, benchmarking means measures of possible performance against other, already existing, products and services. Such comparisons need not be with organizations that precisely match your own. (It is not easy to get benchmark information on your competitors!)

When Xerox wanted to improve its supply and distribution systems, it benchmarked its own systems against those of the outdoors catalog company, L.L. Bean.

Although benchmarking sounds to some people like a tempting shortcut to breakthrough ideas, it really requires a great deal of preparation, execution, and analysis—beginning with a thorough understanding of your own company's process performance and your own customers' requirements.

CAPABILITY PERFORMANCE

If customers require near perfection, our products and services should operate at the Six Sigma level. No matter what the level of customer quality requirement might be, we need to be able to predict and measure the capability of the new product and process. How well will the new product perform? What are the weakest links in the manufacturing process? Where will the face-to-face contacts with customers break down? In part the answers to these questions are informed guesses by experienced experts.

But performance capability can also be based on careful predictions, benchmarks, and estimated measures in the form of performance scorecards. Unlike scorecards in sports, which tell you what has already happened, capability scorecards predict future performance based on estimates of defects at crucial points in the process or manufacture of a product. Like Failure Mode and Effects Analysis, Capability Analysis asks the questions, "What can go wrong? How likely is it that defects will actually occur? Where in the process are failures most likely to occur?" Having these estimates ready in the Measure phase of DFSS will provide performance measures later when the team designs experiments to come up with good products and solutions.

TOOLS USED IN THE ANALYZE PHASE

TRIZ OR INVENTIVE PROBLEM SOLVING

Sooner or later, DFSS teams must face the challenge of contradictory customer requirements and the constraints of their own design concepts. Customers want furniture that is strong but lightweight. Or they want a medical test that is fast, but 100-percent accurate. Instead of seeing these requirements as irreconcilable "either...or" problems, a brainstorming method called TRIZ offers the hope of using contradictions as a source of innovative "both...and" solutions. TRIZ starts with the assumption that such contradictions actually stimulate creative thinking, and TRIZ also offers a large set of inventive principles to enhance that creativity. Here are just a few of these principles in the form of questions:

- What happens if we break the object into smaller components?
- What happens if we strip away most of the components?
- What happens if we merge several functions at the same time?
- How could this object become "self-correcting" when something broke?

TRIZ is the Russian acronym for "Theory of Inventive Problem Solving." It is a structured method for brainstorming. TRIZ provides a series of structured categories for brainstorming, such as the instrument must be precise and easy to use; a questionnaire must be complete and completed within a minute.

PROCESS SIMULATION

Process simulation is often performed with the help of software tools that bring together your process map and processing data, allowing you to automate the statistical tasks associated with analyzing the robustness of the new design and the method by which it will be deployed. Simulation tests the efficiency of the new product's design process, taking into account such measures as cycle time, resource needs, related costs, and yields. Equally important, it gives you a sense as to the Sigma level you will achieve by assessing the error rates of the new offering.

Software simulation packages provide users with an inexpensive way to try to refine a design, using both "as-is" and "what-if" evaluation criteria as shown in this box.

MEASURES FOR SIMULATION

Workflow
    Current or Potential Task
    Concurrency
    Decisions (Percent of flow/path)
    Cycle Time
    Elapsed/Working

Value
    Adding/Enabling
    Non Value Add

Materials
    Cost per Unit

People
    Cost (Standard Rates, Overtime Rates)
    Supervision
    Schedule

Equipment
    Amortization
    Maintenance Costs
    Availability (Uptime)

Setup
    One time or recurring
    Cost per Unit (or Per Incident)

It's important to remember that software simulation tools allow you to easily test variables in a process, but the results are only as good as your own assumptions about how things will work, making the early Design assumptions in DMADV very important.

TOOLS FOR THE DESIGN PHASE

ADVANCED IDEA GENERATION

As customer feedback is being gathered and requirements analyzed, it's important to verify that the assumptions embedded in what we actually deliver to customers are on target. There are a number of approaches that help uncover and modify these assumptions should they be faulty. How they will be applied depends on whether you are conducting a complete overhaul of an existing offering, or whether you are creating these products and services for the first time based on assumed customer requirements and specifications.

Incidentally, our belief is that new products and services are actually inherent in existing products, services, and even in the specifications we've identified for our customers. Here are the 10 categories of questions you should ask that will verify or challenge your assumptions.

1. **Adapt**: How can we adapt existing products or services to our own creation? For example, how can we make a visit to the hospital more like a visit to a luxury hotel?

2. **Modify:** How might a combination of small changes affect our creation? What if we change the tone of the color in an advertisement, as well as doubling its size, changing the font, and changing the illustration?

3. **Substitute:** What other parts might we substitute for existing ones in a device? What other process could we substitute for one already in place? Can we substitute a supplier's process for one of our own?

4. **Add On:** What might be added to a product to strengthen it? Weaken it? Should we add a step to prevent problems downstream in a process? What additional features are required to meet new customer specifications?

5. **Maximize:** What happens if we double the size of our product? If we double the number of services offered by our call center? What happens if we increase the price of our product? How can we maximize the power of our product?

6. **Minimize:** What would a miniature version of our product look like? What if our current 30-step sales process were reduced to 3 steps? What if the price of our service were only a fraction of what it is today? Can we leave out two inspections? How do we minimize the number of approvals required?

7. **Division:** What happens if we divide our product into smaller units? Can our service be divided into many easier steps? Can we split the costs of our service with our suppliers?

8. **Rearrange:** Mark Twain wondered what life would be like if we were born old and frail and got younger and stronger every day. Quite a rearrangement of the normal process! What happens to your process if the steps in it were reversed? Or if they took place in a random order?

9. **Combine:** DFSS strives to offer customers the power inherent in the "both…and" approach to products and service, rather than "either…or," meaning that we want to offer them speed *and* accuracy rather than offering them a dismal choice of one or the other. How can we combine process steps to increase efficiency and effectiveness? Wacky though it might be, a recent combination appeared in a talking bottle opener that treated users to a speech from Homer Simpson when it was used!

10. **Dependency:** How can we make features of our product or service dependent on one another in new ways that would meet customer specifications? Domino's Pizza made a fortune by making the price of its delivered pizza dependent on meeting a promised delivery time. Could another entrepreneur offer a similar dependency between temperature of the pizza at delivery time and price? One of our clients improved the quality of its service to its customers when it changed the dependency of the telemarketers' bonus from speed to accuracy and a balance between the two.

And the list might be extended indefinitely. There are many, many ways to challenge assumptions and begin to create tangible products and services as a by-product of those challenges. By now you should have a number of raw ideas that need some maturing and synthesizing. If this process was performed correctly, you should have a laundry list of ideas that can be narrowed down to the top three or four possibilities, the next step in the Design phase.

Narrowing down raw ideas involves the following steps:

- Combine related ideas and begin to eliminate obviously fanciful nonstarters.
- Link your creative solutions to customer specifications identified in the Measure and Analyze phases.
- Use the results of these two steps to write a complete description of the new products or services.

It's possible that one clear winner has emerged from your brainstorming, challenging, and narrowing efforts. More often you'll have to choose among several candidates, each with its own positive and negative features, each with its own risks. It's time now to actually begin selecting the best of the bunch. Remember that even as we're deciding, we'll still be looking for ways to improve our choice.

Obviously, our choices should meet customer requirements and promise the lowest amount of variation and highest predictability possible. We'll also have to assess our costs and the impact of the various choices. We'll look for a balance between the two, so that the greater the effort to implement the solution, the greater the expected impact.

Where the impact of the new process will be great or where there will be strong opposition from key stakeholders, it's a good idea to do a more formal comparison and analysis of the solutions. There are a number of such analyses, all of which consist of a matrix in which alternatives are rated against ranked criteria to come up with weighted scores. The process of comparing alternative solutions against customer specifications will reveal that the solutions vary in their ability to meet the specs. No matter which alternative comes up with the highest score, it is worth reviewing the other choices to see if elements of them might still be incorporated in the "heaviest" choice.

PUGH MATRIX

The Pugh Matrix (also known as Criteria Based Matrix and Decision Matrix method) will help establish which product features are more important than others relative to the customer requirements identified earlier in the project. This scoring matrix is an important tool during the Design phase and is used to rank options by comparing concepts according to their strengths or weaknesses relative to the desired features of the product, service, or process (see Figure 7.2).

The Pugh Matrix works well when each DFSS team member does her own ranking of alternate concepts and then compares results with other team members.

DESIGN OF EXPERIMENTS

As its name suggests, Design of Experiments (DoE) involves setting up an experiment to test a new design. Experiments are purposeful changes of the various factors in an attempt to discover their relationship to the outcome, or to find the most optimum settings for best performance. Designed experiments rely on a fairly advanced set of statistical analysis tools to interpret the results, but they are grounded on a foundation of logic and build on the principles of good measurement.

We consider Designed Experiments for several reasons:

- Identify factors that affect process performance.
- Optimize product/process performance.
- Minimize variability to achieve robust design.
- Obtain the most information in the least amount of time and for the least expense.

And it is applicable to:

- Existing process and products
- New process and product designs

	CONCEPTS							
KEY CRITERIA	Concept 1 New Design	Concept 2 Use Existing Datum	Concept 3 Copy C.C. Bank	Concept 4	Concept 5	Concept 6	Concept 7	Importance Rating
Ability to Provide Loan Amount	S	S	–					3
Interest Rate	S	S	–					2
Application Time	S	S	S					5
Knowledgeable Representatives	+	S	+					1
Availability of Representatives	+	S	–					4
Information Requirements	+	S	–					3
Processing Time	–	S	–					5
Cost/Transaction	+	S	–					3
Defects/Transaction	S	S	–					3
Development Budget	–	S	+					5
Sum of Positives	4	0	2					
Sum of Negatives	2	0	7					
Sum of Sames	4	10	1					
Weighted Sum of Positives	11	0	6					
Weighted Sum of Negatives	10	0	23					

Concept Selection Legend
Better   +
Same   S
Worse   –

Analysis: Concept 3's negatives outweigh its positives and should be dropped from further consideration. Concept 1 has a slight edge over the datum, but is not a clear winner. More thought should go into refining/improving this concept.

FIGURE 7.2. The Pugh Matrix.

Remember in middle school when we were asked to conduct some simple experiment—testing the effects of sunlight, water, and soil on the growth of bean seeds, for instance. Those were "One Factor at a Time" experiments—you changed only one variable at a time (for instance amount of sunlight) on each tray of seeds, and the results were generally obvious. What we missed were the possible interactions of two or more of the factors—what happens when both sunlight and water are changed? Testing one factor or variable at a time ignores these interactions.

Before we talk about how an experiment is set up and the results interpreted, let's identify some different situations and types of designs. Essentially there are three categories of designs—Factorials, Mixture, and Response Surface designs, each with their specific applications. Certain industries seem to favor specific design types. For instance, many automotive suppliers favor Taguchi designs, although there is much dispute about which is "best" within a particular category.

Designed Experiments are also catalogued by their purpose, either screening or optimization. Screening experiments separate the factors that have a significant influence on the response from the rest of the factors. Often screening designs are a prelude to further experiments.

Response Surface Designs were invented to find the optimal response within the specified ranges of the factors. The results of the analysis of these experiments are typically displayed as a three-dimensional surface, showing the optimum conditions.

DESIGN TYPES

- Factorial designs, including Taguchi: for assessing the impact of a few to several X's (factors) on a Y (response). (The goal of the Taguchi Method is to find control factor settings that generate acceptable responses despite natural environmental and process variability.)

- Mixture designs: for determining the right proportion of ingredients in a mixture—think of determining how much flour, sugar, and butter to put in dough to get cookies.

- Response Surface designs: for optimizing the settings of a very limited number of X's for a couple of Y's.

FAILURE MODES AND EFFECTS ANALYSIS (FMEA)

Identifying and managing risk is critical to a successful design, and a very effective and popular tool is FMEA. Developed by the Military and Aerospace industries, it is typically used several times during a DFSS project. In addition to making the design more robust, FMEA is often used to manage risks associated with collecting VoC in the Define phase, ("We're going to do a survey, what could go wrong?") and again prior to piloting or implementation ("Let's consider what could go wrong during our pilot").

Working from left to right across the FMEA form (Figure 7-3), an FMEA begins with identification of every conceivable "failure mode"—problems, or ways that the design could break, injure someone, or fail to meet a CTQ. Each of these failure modes can have a variety of consequences, perhaps of different severities, which are identified and assigned a severity rating. Effects unlikely to result in damage typically get a score of 1, and those resulting in severe injury or death a score of 10.

STEPS TO DOE

1. Description of expected learnings
2. Identification of the response variable
3. Selection of test factors and levels
4. Cataloging of noise variables
5. Construction of experimental approach and design
6. Measurement system analysis
7. Perform the experiment
8. Analyze the results
9. Conclusions and recommendations
10. Possibly narrow and repeat

FMEA Worksheet

Project or Person: _____

Process, Product, Service: _____

Date: _____

Feature or Step	Failure Mode	Effect/Impact (severity data)	Cause(s) (occurrence data)	Controls/Measures (detection data)	RATINGS			RPN S x O x D	RESPONSES		
					S	O	D		Action	Who	When

FIGURE 7.3. FMEA worksheet.

For each effect, a determination is made of the likelihood of occurrence (10 = very likely or frequent, 1 = not likely), and then an assessment of the current controls or discovery methods is used to assign a detectability rating (10 = undetectable until the damage is done, 1 = obvious).

These three scores are multiplied together to generate associated risk priority numbers (ranging from 1 to 1000) that establish the sequence for managing the identified risks.

Focusing first on prevention, next early detection, then mitigation (or damage control), the team modifies the design as necessary and assesses the new and revised failure modes to ensure a safe, reliable product or process.

TOOLS FOR THE VERIFY PHASE

PROCESS DOCUMENTATION AND MONITORING

Used in the final stages of a DMAIC initiative, process documentation takes on a different view in the Verify phase of DFSS. Here it is the final opportunity to ensure that the quality designed into the new offering will be sustained. Control Plans document the crucial characteristics and requirements of the design and address the design team's efforts to eliminate defects from their design, establish a means of identifying defects should they occur, and institute a plan for eradicating these defects. Control Charts are effective ways for monitoring any changes in the design process going forward, distinguishing between changes that are bound to happen (common cause) and those variations that will result in a change in the process and/or design (special cause).

Statistical Process Control (SPC) is one such documentation approach. In SPC, the DFSS team applies statistical tools to check process capability and performance. Typical SPC tools include flow charts, Pareto charts, cause-and-effect diagrams, and scatter diagrams, in addition to control charts noted above.

RESPONSE PLANNING

Response Planning makes sure there are no surprises waiting for the DFSS team; it helps the team take a more proactive approach to anticipating the need for corrective action, and predetermining their actions in the event of a problem or excess variation. It has a response or action ready should the monitoring system detect possible defects.

Typically, before a team began its Six Sigma adventure, each event was a new fire drill—frequently requiring management's intervention to solve known problems over and over again. Response planning entails performing a Failure Modes and Effects Analysis (FMEA)—or updating one done earlier—to predict and prioritize potential problems and then make a response plan for each. Response plans typically address:

- Damage Control—What can done immediately upon detection of the event to limit further damage?
- Process Adjustment—What changes to the process will put things back on track?
- Assess Effectiveness—Verify that the adjustment has restored capability.
- Continuous Improvement—Document the learnings for future improvement activities.

The payoff is the right kind of response to the specific issue or problem, and avoidance of tampering (making process changes that aren't warranted) or missing an opportunity to correct a problem. Good response demands both the right alarm settings and the right response plans. It's all about timely, effective *action*.

PROCESS MANAGEMENT

Process Dashboards and Balanced Scorecards are two popular methods of verifying the effectiveness of your design over the life of the product or service. They provide a summary of the crucial measures built into the design to enable real-time feedback and promote prompt attention to problems or opportunities. These tools typically feature both output (Y) and input (X) measures and extend well beyond traditional financial data.

SUMMARY

In our previous book, *What is Six Sigma?*, we stressed the importance of applying Six Sigma tools judiciously. In our work we have found that using too many tools or overcomplicating their use can be just as damaging as using no tools at all. We offer the same advice to DFSS teams, when using tools:

1. Use only those that help you get the job done.
2. Keep things simple.
3. Admit when a tool isn't helping, and try something else.

Now that you have an understanding of the process, how and when it is applied, and the tools to use during a DFSS project, the following chapters offer practical tips for managers championing a DFSS effort and the teams executing the project.

A NOTE TO MANAGERS: HOW YOU CAN HELP LEAD THE DFSS PROCESS

Once you're committed to one DFSS path or the other, the real work of making change is up to you and a whole crew of business leaders, team members, team leaders, and facilitators familiar with the DFSS process. Some of these people will have titles like Black Belt, Master Black Belt, Green Belt, and Champion. If you're already familiar with these roles from earlier Six Sigma experience, they have similar functions in DFSS.

In this chapter, we define these titles and their job functions. Take special note of the Champion entry; it is our hope that the information in this book will create Champions at all levels of the Six Sigma organization. The final sections discuss these opportunities and the pros and cons Champions face in their role as team leader or manager. Throughout we offer tips and advice for managing the project and the project team during what can sometimes seem an arduous process.

BLACK BELT

The role of the Black Belt in DFSS is probably the most crucial one. The Black Belt is a full-time internal consultant devoted to driving DFSS projects to successful conclusion. The Black Belt leads, teaches, manages, delegates, and coaches team members and others touched by the DFSS project. The Black Belt usually works alongside a team tasked with overhauling a core process or creating a new product. He or she initiates the team, often joining the team during its training, supporting it throughout the DFSS project, guiding the team as it applies DFSS tools, and generally steering the entire effort toward a successful, profitable conclusion.

The successful Black Belt working on a DFSS project must have many skills. He or she must have a high tolerance for ambiguity, particularly in the earliest stages of a DFSS project when the outcome is very uncertain. Indeed, the Black Belt has to help maintain that level of tolerance lest the team settle for a 90-percent improvement or release a new product that has bugs in it. The Black Belt is a mixture of blue-sky innovator and hard-nosed project manager, helping the team go from wild-eyed brainstorms to rock-solid improvements, complete with documented measures of success. Often drawn from the ranks of middle management, Black Belts usually perform these functions for two years, during which they may complete one or two major DFSS projects.

MASTER BLACK BELT

With several projects under their belt, proven analytical skills, and often advanced degrees in business, Master Black Belts have the job of assisting and supporting several Black Belts and DFSS projects. Because of their experience, Master Black Belts often play the role of change agent, actively supporting and campaigning for specific DFSS projects and management goals. They might also be actively engaged in working directly with important customers, identifying their crucial requirements and helping the DFSS team build a process or product that meets those requirements near to or at the Six Sigma level.

The Master Black Belt will make sure that the team reaches its interim goals by passing a series of tollgate reviews—key tasks that must be completed in each stage of the DFSS process. The Master Black Belt is usually heavily involved in the measurement of financial results, and in the selling of new solutions to other

---

Top Five Black Belt Characteristics

In addition to being a strong team leader and possessing exceptional technical aptitude and business acumen, Black Belts must also excel in the following five roles:

Customer Advocate: CTQs are the key to process improvement. Black Belts effectively determine the customer's CTQs and convey them to the DFSS team.

Team Motivator: Black Belts are often the drivers in their DFSS teams; they are self-motivated, results-oriented, and a positive influence.

Change Agent: Black Belts embrace the notion of change and lead their team through processes that lead to effective change within the organization, whether it be to a core process, strategy, product, or solution.

Clear Communicator: Whether the interactions are external or internal to the organization with customers or board directors, Black Belts must be articulate, persuasive, forthright communicators.

Project Manager: Black Belts need to monitor every aspect of the project, from resources to results, with exceptional focus and clarity.

Adapted from "Top Ten Six Sigma Black Belt Candidate Qualities," Charles Waxer, isixsigma.com, 3/17/03.

---

people in the organization. Above all, the role of the Master Black Belt in DFSS projects is to push for genuine breakthrough solutions that perform at the best possible level in meeting customer requirements.

GREEN BELT

Green Belts form the bulk of the Six Sigma team and have undergone training for DFSS. However, unlike Black Belts, the DFSS project is only part of a Green Belt's life, while continuing to do her regular job.

CHAMPION

DFSS and Six Sigma Champions come from all levels of the company; they are troubleshooters, problem solvers, and advocates for the project. They are mediators, defusing issues that might arise between members of the DFSS team, and professionals who influence without the necessary job title, convincing management of the goals and value of a particular DFSS initiative.

In some organizations, DuPont for example, the Champion is a very senior member of the organization; however, seniority isn't necessarily a mandate. Very often, the Champion is the liaison between the DFSS team and the company's Vice Presidents, Officers, and Directors.

Champions must be equally skilled in areas of diplomacy, strategy, and execution so that they are able to align business goals with operations, identify and select those projects that will be the most valuable to the firm, monitor the resources and costs of the DFSS project, and incorporate the team's findings into the product, service, or core process being designed.

WORKING WITH THE DFSS EXPERTS

Managers working on a DFSS project in any of the capacities cited above have the opportunity with every phase of the effort and every interaction to enhance their own managerial and leadership skills by both exerting authority appropriately and learning from customers and fellow team members.

TIPS FOR MANAGERS

Identify and align yourself with a Champion.
Institute programs that will reshape culture and behavior.
Create opportunities that will involve employees.
Prevent exceptions to the process.

For managers, we recommend the following in order to both build professional leadership skills and effectively manage a DFSS project to fruition.

Find a Champion

As we discussed above, a Six Sigma Champion is a committed advocate to the approach and to projects that will positively impact the company. Whether it is an improvement in the company's product or services, or to an internal process or strategy, finding an advocate who has been an effective influencer within the organization is essential. For many firms, advocates are often responsible for the financial results of the company, either as sales or marketing executives, CIOs, or COOs. If the DFSS project is focusing on an internal process or strategy, your Champion might be found among the officers and directors of the company. As noted in Chapter 2, those companies who have achieved unparalleled success with their Six Sigma programs have had support at the CEO level of the organization.

Modify Organizational Behavior

GE is famous for saying that Six Sigma is a part of the organization's DNA. This type of companywide acceptance will make both the job of the manager and Champion much, much easier—but alas, these companies are rare. There exists then an opportunity to persuade groups within the organization of the value of a DFSS effort. This conversion is much more essential obviously if the DFSS project is focusing on changing an aspect of the company's strategy or process.

Involve Employees

It is much easier to modify organizational behavior by involving employees in the project. If you are implementing a new technology system for your firm, bring the employees who will actually use the system into the process. If your group is changing the structure of your firm's back-office operations, see how divisions all over the firm will be impacted as well as those directly involved.

PREVENT PROCESS EXCEPTIONS

Much like the Black Belt's astute sense of project management and technical skill, managers must closely monitor the process to avoid introducing flaws and losing productivity. Once you have determined the course of your DFSS project in the earliest stages of the DMADV method, stick to it.

CHAPTER 9

A NOTE TO DFSS TEAM MEMBERS

If Six Sigma and DFSS have arrived, or are on the horizon, at your organization, you can expect some changes and opportunities to come your way.[1] Beyond understanding the basic approach to DFSS, the next question you're likely to ask is "How can I make a DFSS project a positive experience for me?" So here are some tips and hints that will make you better prepared to thrive in a Six Sigma organization.

1. Learn the goals and objectives of the DFSS effort. Each company has a somewhat different perspective on why Six Sigma is needed and what it will help achieve. Listen and look for communications about the initiative's vision, plans for teams, training, scale, speed, roles, and responsibilities. All this will help you anticipate what you can do—or what you'll be asked to do—to contribute to the Six Sigma change.

2. Prepare for some confusion. Six Sigma might be a goal of near-perfect performance, but performing DFSS in a business is never perfect, particularly given that you are instituting radical change rather than incremental improvements. This means you can expect plans to change, roles to evolve, signals to get crossed, projects to be launched and revamped or abandoned. This is all a part of the messy job of organizational change. Hopefully in your company, the messiness will be kept to a minimum—but some of it is inevitable and you should not let it discourage you from learning and benefiting from the DFSS effort.

[1] This chapter is adapted from our book *What Is Six Sigma?*, pages 81-86.

3. Begin looking at your work from a "SIPOC" point of view. You can get a head start on practicing the concepts of Six Sigma and DFSS if you think of your job as part of a chain of activities: Suppliers and Inputs (the things you rely on), Process (the work you and your colleagues do), and Outputs and Customers (the final product and people who receive it). Ask yourself some important questions: Do I understand what my/our customers really need? (And do they?) How well are we meeting their needs? Is our process well organized and efficient—or confused and rework ridden? How well have we conveyed our needs to suppliers? (Remember, these might be people in your company.) This does not have to be a detailed analysis, but it might give you ideas for DFSS projects—and a chance to see how its principles can make your life easier and your job more productive.

4. Take advantage of learning opportunities. DFSS training can be challenging, but it's also full of great ideas and tools that can help you in your daily life as well as at work. So if you get a chance to be involved in awareness training, Green Belt courses, or even to become a Black Belt, your best bet is to go into it expecting to work hard and gain a lot.

5. Avoid paranoia. One of the biggest hindrances to success in Six Sigma—for an individual or a business—comes from fear and worry. Sometimes, it's just fear of change; in other cases, it is worry that you will be blamed for the very problems being analyzed. It can even happen that Black Belts or DFSS teams will be afraid to point out concerns to their project Champion. But remember, the driving force behind DFSS is acknowledging that problems exist, whether in a process, existing product design, or even in a company's performance. If you look at the DFSS effort as a positive opportunity to make things better, it has a much greater chance of success than if you approach Six Sigma as your albatross.

6. Expect changes and challenges to come. When we say to avoid fear and paranoia, we don't mean you should not anticipate some disruptions and challenges. As we've

described, participating in a DFSS project usually requires some sacrifice. Adopting new procedures and living by new processes is hard if you are comfortable with the way you've always done things. Changes might even mean people being reassigned or given brand new roles. And, yes, sometimes these projects lead to people being laid off—if it's determined that this is one of the ways a company can be more efficient. Usually, however, even the most painful changes are made for good reasons—not just as some blind effort to save money.

7. Take responsibility for your own learning. We use this phrase a lot in training programs. It's not a trainer's cop-out, though. It simply means "Be proactive in finding out what you need and want to know." Asking questions, reading books and articles, talking to people involved in Six Sigma and DFSS teams, attending informational meetings, using chat rooms or e-mail contacts—these should all be part of your effort to learn and understand more about Six Sigma. Remember, some answers will be tentative—but there are few organizations where you can't learn more if you try.

8. Volunteer, be patient, and don't get discouraged. Sounds like a mix of suggestions, doesn't it? But these are related: First of all, if you feel eager, ready, and enthusiastic about getting actively involved in a DFSS effort, let your manager or other key people know. If you have project ideas, send them along. On the other hand, remember that your company or division might have more participants than it can handle—so your offer might not lead to immediate assignment to a DFSS team. Even the most aggressive Six Sigma rollouts can't get everyone involved right away—so if you are only on the outskirts of Six Sigma for a while, hang in there.

9. Be ready for the long haul! Companies let past improvement initiatives dwindle away because they never really became ingrained in the management processes. Six Sigma and DFSS holds the promise of having a significant impact on the organization, as the examples in Chapter 2 demonstrate.

THE FIVE SKILLS YOU'LL NEED

The skills you will need to participate successfully in a DFSS initiative can be developed by any team member regardless of prior Six Sigma experience. Here are the five most important ones:

SKILL #1: The ability to see the big picture. Being an expert in your own field or functional area is fine. But reaching Six Sigma performance relies on people who can see and understand a process from end to end. So-called "empowered" people in a Six Sigma company will be those with the broader view and ability to make decisions based on what works for the end customer and the whole process.

SKILL #2: The ability to gather data. Gathering data does not mean statistical wizardry. It's about being able to separate factual observation from opinion and guess—and record or explain the facts accurately. There's a saying that's been around for quite a few years: "In God we Trust—all others bring data." This is even more applicable in a DFSS world.

SKILL #3: The ability to break through old assumptions. The biggest unseen obstacles to improving your business are probably the current beliefs on things like: "What our customers care about." "How important this task is." "That's something we could never afford," or " We have the best process in the industry." Many of these assumptions turn out to be wrong. Holding on to these beliefs freezes change and invites complacency. Today, complacency in business is frequently a terminal disease.

SKILL #4: The ability to work collaboratively. DFSS projects and results have repeatedly proven that a "win-win" approach creates more value for everyone than a "win-lose." Along with the ability to see the big picture (see Skill 1), you'll have to be comfortable with using that understanding to find better ways to team up, share, take responsibility, listen, value other opinions, and develop solutions that work for the greatest benefit—usually starting with benefits to external customers. This is what GE Chairman Jack Welch has called a "boundaryless" organization.

SKILL #5: The ability to thrive on change. There is no way around change; it is going to happen whether you like it or not. Change for no good reason is bad, of course, but change that makes you and your coworkers better able to get the right things done is terrific. The most important skill overall in Six Sigma and DFSS is just that: making change work for you, your customers and your organization.

There are no simple ways to develop these five key skills. Most of them start with your attitude. We hope that in the lessons you've learned in this book, you can feel the sense of optimism and energy we see in the companies where Six Sigma is making an impact. If you do, you'll be starting with the right attitude needed to develop these skills.

GLOSSARY OF SIX SIGMA TERMS

Affinity Diagram
Brainstorming tool used to gather large quantities of information from many people; ideas are usually put on sticky notes, then categorized into similar columns; columns are named giving an overall grouping of ideas.

Analyze
DMADV phase where high-level conceptual designs are created and evaluated. DMAIC phase where data is analyzed and the process scrutinized to determine root causes.

Black Belt
A team leader trained in the DMADV process and facilitation skills; responsible for guiding an improvement project to completion.

Brainstorming
An open, free-flowing technique for collecting ideas from a variety of individuals; rules include: no ideas are considered "dumb;" no judgments, discussions, or clarifications until all ideas are generated; the wilder the better.

Capability
The performance of a process versus customer requirements. A process with a lot of variation won't be capable of consistently meeting customer needs.

Cause and Effect Diagram
Also known as a Fishbone or Ishikawa Diagram; categorical brainstorming tool used for determining root-cause hypothesis

and potential causes (the bones of the fish) for a specific effect (the head of the fish).

Charter
Team document defining the context, specifics, and plans of a design project; includes business case, problem and goal statements, constraints and assumptions, roles, preliminary plan, and scope. Periodic reviews with the sponsor ensure alignment with business strategies; review, revise, refine periodically throughout the DMADV process based on data.

Checksheet
Forms, tables, or worksheets used for data collection and compilation; allows for collection of stratified data (see Stratification).

Coach
Trained, experienced Black Belt who helps to guide newer Black Belts and improvement teams. Responsible for introducing quality tools and concepts to improvement teams and the organization

Critical to Quality (CTQs)
Those characteristics of the output that determine its usability to the customer, or customer's specific quality requirements.

Customer
Any internal or external person/organization who receives and uses the output (product or service) of the process; understanding the impact of the process on both internal and external customers is key to process management and improvement. The customer determines the quality of a product or service.

Customer Focus (Voice of the Customer)
An emphasis on, and the ability to: 1) identify and verify current customer needs, 2) anticipate future needs, and 3) look for opportunities to add value to the customer; balance of customer retention and acquisition

Customer Requirements

Define the needs and expectations of the customer; translated into measurable terms and used in the process to ensure compliance to the customers' needs.

Cycle Time

All time used in a process; includes actual work time and wait time.

Defect

Any failure of a product or service to meet customer requirements.

Defect Opportunity

Any chance for failure to meet customer requirements. A type of potential defect on a unit of throughput (output) that is important to the customer; example: specific fields on a form that creates an opportunity for error that would be important to the customer. If the total # of fields is 40 but only 6 fields are crucial to the customer, count only 6 defect opportunities; defects per opportunity is used when calculating DPO and DPMO for Six Sigma performance (see also Defect, DPMO, DPO, Six Sigma).

Defective

Any unit with one or more defects (see Defects).

Define

First DMADV phase (D); defines the opportunity, process, and customer requirements (see Charter, Customer Requirements, Process Map, VOC).

Design for Six Sigma (DFSS)

DFSS is a process for building quality into products and services at a Six Sigma level.

Design of Experiments (DoE)

DoE is a structured, organized method for determining the relationship between factors (Xs) affecting a process and the output of that process (Y).

DMAIC
Acronym for process improvement/management system that stands for Define, Measure, Analyze, Improve, and Control; lends structure to process improvement, design, or redesign applications.

DMADV
Acronym for the most commonly used model for guiding Design for Six Sigma projects. Stands for Define, Measure, Analyze, Design, and Verify. Variations include DMADOV, DCCDI, IDOV, DMEDI.

DPMO, Defects per Million Opportunities
Calculation used in Six Sigma process improvement initiatives indicating the amount of defects in a process per one million opportunities; # of defects divided by (the # of units times the # of opportunities) = DPO, times 1 million = DPMO (see also DPO, Six Sigma, Defect Opportunity).

DPO, Defects per Opportunity
Calculation used in process improvements to determine the amount of defects per opportunity; # of defects divided by (the # of units times the # of opportunities) = DPO (see also Defect, Defect Opportunity).

Entitlement
The best that a product or process can perform, after improvements, and under ideal circumstances, but without a redesign.

Facilitator
An individual or role. Responsible for ensuring that a meeting or discussion progresses effectively with all viewpoints considered; may be a team member, leader, or outside individual.

FMEA (Failure Modes and Effects Analysis)
A risk-management tool for assessing the relative priority of possible problems or failure modes, considering their Severity, Occurrence, and Detectability. Used for planning appropriate action.

Force Field Analysis
Identifies forces/factors supporting or working against an idea; "restraining" factors listed on one side of the page—"driving forces" listed on the other; used to reinforce the strengths (positive ideas) and overcome the weaknesses or obstacles.

Goal Statement
Description of the intended target or desired results of process improvement activities; usually written in verb/noun structure; does not suggest causes, solutions, or blame; usually included in a team charter and supported with actual numbers and details once data is obtained and usually includes a target date; e.g., 1) Reduce cycle time in the billing process. 2) Reduce accounts receivables billing cycle by 30 percent before December 31, 2005. (See also Charter.)

Greenfield Design
A completely new design (think of a bulldozer clearing a green field for a new building) as opposed to a redesign.

Handoff
Any time in a process where one person (or job title) passes the item moving through the process to another person; potential to add defects, time, and cost to a process.

Histogram
Chart used to summarize process data for a period of time; graphically represents the frequency and distribution of the data.

House of Quality (Quality Function Deployment or QFD)
A series of interlocking matrices that bring the CTQs together with competitive and technical benchmark information to deliver performance targets for the new design.

Improve
DMAIC phase (I) where solutions and ideas are brainstormed, selected, and mistake-proofed against possible failures.

Once a problem is fully identified, measured, and analyzed, potential solutions can be determined to solve the problem statement and support the goal statement (see Charter).

Input
Any product, service, or information that comes into the process from a supplier.

Input Measures
Measures related to and describing the input into a process; predictors of output.

Measure
DMADV phase where the future measures of success (and their tolerances) are developed.

DMAIC phase (M) where key measures are identified and data is collected, compiled, and displayed.

A quantified evaluation of specific characteristics and/or level of performance based on observable data.

Multivoting
Narrowing and prioritization tool. Faced with a list or ideas, problems, causes, etc., each member of a group is given a set number of "votes." Those receiving most votes get further attention/consideration

Non-Value-Adding Activities
Steps/tasks in a process that do not add value to the external customer and do not meet all three criteria for value-adding; includes rework, handoffs, inspection/control, wait/delays, etc. (See Value-Adding Activities.)

Opportunity Statement
A description of the opportunity to be filled by this design effort, not including a specific solution or design. Usually a leading element of the Charter.

Output
Any product, service, or information coming out of, or resulting from, the activities in a process.

Output Measures
Measures related to and describing the output of the process; total figures/overall measures.

Pareto Chart
Quality tool based on Pareto Principle; uses attribute data with columns arranged in descending order, with highest occurrences (highest bar) shown first; uses a cumulative line to track percentages of each category/bar, which distinguishes the 20 percent of items causing 80 percent of the problem.

Pareto Principle
The 80/20 rule; based on Vilfredo Pareto's research stating that the vital few (20 percent) of causes have a greater impact than the trivial many (80 percent) causes with a lesser impact.

Pilot
Trial implementation of a solution, on a limited scale, to ensure its effectiveness and test its impact; an experiment verifying root cause hypothesis.

Preliminary Plan
Used when developing milestones for team activities related to process improvement; includes key tasks, target completion dates, responsibilities, potential problems, obstacles and contingencies, and communication strategies.

Problem
Negative variation of a product or process from customer requirements, often with unknown causes.

Problem Statement
Description of the symptoms, or the "pain" in the process; usually written in noun/verb structure; does not suggest causes, solutions, or blame; usually included in a team charter and supported with numbers and more detail once data is obtained; 1) The billing cycle takes too long. 2) The account receivables billing cycle takes an average of 43 days. (See also Charter.)

Process
A series of steps whereby one thing (input) becomes another thing (output).

Process Capability
Determination of whether or not a process, with normal variation, is capable of meeting customer requirements; measure of the degree a process is/is not meeting customer requirements, compared to the distribution of the process (see Control, Control Charts).

Process Improvement
Improvement approach focused on incremental changes/solutions to eliminate or reduce defects, costs, or cycle time; leaves basic design and assumptions of a process intact (see Process Redesign).

Process Management
Defined and documented processes, monitored on an ongoing basis, that ensure that measures are providing feedback on the flow/function of a process; key measures include financial, process, people, innovation (see Control).

Process Map or Flowchart
Graphic display of the process flow that shows all activities, decision points, rework loops, and handoffs.

Process Measures
Measures related to individual steps as well as total process; predictors of output measures.

Process Redesign
Method of restructuring process flow elements eliminating handoffs, rework loops, inspection points, and other non-value-added activities; typically means "clean slate" design of a business segment and accommodates major changes or yields exponential improvements (similar to reengineering). (See Process Improvement, Reengineering.)

QFD (Quality Function Deployment)
See "House of Quality."

Quality
A broad concept and/or discipline involving degree of excellence; a distinguished attribute or nature; conformance to specifications; measurable standards of comparison so applications can be consistently directed toward business goals.

Rework Loop
Any instance in a process when the thing moving through the process has to be corrected by returning it to a previous step or person/organization in the process; adds time, costs, and potential for confusion and more defects (see also Non-Value-Added Activities).

Run Chart or Time Plot
Measurement display tool showing variation in a factor over time; indicates trends, patterns, and instances of special causes of variation (see Control Chart, Special Cause, Variation).

Sampling
Using a smaller number of units to represent the whole.

Scatter Plot or Diagram
Graph used to show relationship—or correlation—between two factors or variables.

Scope
Defines the boundaries of the process or the process improvement project; clarifies specifically where opportunities for improvement reside (start and end points); defines where and what to measure and analyze; needs to be within the sphere of influence and control of the team working on the project. The broader the scope, the more complex and time-consuming process improvement efforts will be.

Scribe
Role of a team member to record ideas and comments on a flip chart or white board during a meeting.

Should-Be Process Mapping
Process mapping approach showing the design of a process the way it *should* be (e.g., without non-value-added activities, with streamlined workflow and new solutions incorporated). Contrasts with the "As-Is" form of process mapping (see also Process Redesign, Value Added, Non-Value-Added Activities).

SIPOC
Acronym for: Suppliers, Inputs, Process, Outputs, and Customer; enables an "at-a-glance" high-level view of a process.

Sigma
Stands for the statistical concept of standard deviation.

Six Sigma
1) Level of process performance equivalent to producing only 3.4 defects for every one million opportunities or operations.
2) Term used to describe process improvement initiatives using sigma-based process measures and/or striving for six sigma-level performance.

Sponsor (Champion)
Person who represents team issues to senior management; gives final approval on team recommendations and supports those efforts with the Quality Council; facilitates obtaining team resources as needed; helps Black Belt and team overcome obstacles; acts as a mentor for the Black Belt.

Stratification
Looking at data in multiple layers of information such as what (types, complaints, etc.), when (month, day, year, etc.), where (region, city, state, etc.), who (department, individual).

Subgroup
The number of consecutive units extracted for measurement at each sampling event; a subgroup can be just one. Subgroup data may be required depending on the size of the population to be sampled, and for specific SPC charts.

Supplier
Any person or organization that feeds, inputs (products, services, or information) into the process; in a service organization, many times the customer is also the supplier.

Taguchi Methods
One of several types of Designed Experiments for determining acceptable controllable factor (Xs) settings despite noise and process variation.

TRIZ
An acronym for the Russian "Theory of Inventive Problem Solving" initially created by Genrich Altshuller in the 1970s. A structured tool for challenging contradictions and constraints.

Value-Adding Activities
Steps/tasks in a process that meet all three criteria defining value as perceived by the external customer: 1) the customer cares, 2) the thing moving through the process changes, and 3) the step is done right the first time.

Variation
Change or fluctuation of a specific characteristic that determines how stable or predictable the process may be; caused by environment, people, machinery/equipment, methods/procedures, measurements and materials; any process improvement should reduce or eliminate variation.

Voice of the Customer (VoC)
The needs, expectations, and performance requirements as gathered from the Customer of the product or process. This VoC will need to be refined and reduced to specific measurable requirements (CTQs).